AI at Home: Transforming Your Child's Learning Experience

First published by Aussie Trading LLC
Copyright © 2025 by Juan Rodulfo
All rights reserved.
No part of this publication may be reproduced, stored, or transmitted in any form or by any means, electronic, mechanical, photocopying, recording, scanning or otherwise without written permission from the publisher. It is illegal to copy this book, publish it on a website, or distribute it by any other means without permission.
Juan Rodulfo has no responsibility for the persistence or accuracy of URLs of external or third-party Internet websites referenced in this publication and does not warrant that the content of such websites is, or will remain, accurate or appropriate.
The names used by companies to distinguish their products are often claimed as trademarks. All trademarks and product names used in this book and on its cover, trade names, service marks, trademarks are trademarks of their respective owners. The publishers and the book are not associated with any products or suppliers mentioned in this book. None of the companies or organizations referenced in the book have endorsed it.
Library of Congress Catalog
Names: Rodulfo, Juan
ISBN: 979-8-3493-3639-3 (e-book)
ISBN: 979-8-3493-3640-9 (paperback)
ISBN: 979-8-3493-3641-6 (hardcover)
First edition
Layout by Juan Rodulfo
Cover art by Guaripete Solutions
Production: Aussie Trading, LLC
books@aussietrading.ltd
Printed in the USA

"AI will not replace humans, but those who use AI will replace those who don't."
Ginni Rometty

Introduction

Artificial Intelligence, commonly referred to as AI, encompasses a range of technologies that enable machines to perform tasks that typically require human intelligence. This includes problem-solving, understanding natural language, recognizing patterns, and learning from experience. In the context of education, AI can be particularly transformative, providing personalized learning experiences that cater to the individual needs of children. By leveraging AI, educational tools can assess a child's progress in real time, adapting content to ensure that learning is both effective and engaging.

At its core, AI operates through algorithms, which are sets of rules or instructions that guide the machine in processing information. These algorithms can analyze vast amounts of data, allowing AI systems to identify trends and make predictions. In educational settings, AI tools can evaluate a child's performance over time, identifying strengths and weaknesses. This data-driven approach enables parents and educators to tailor learning strategies, ensuring that students are challenged appropriately while also receiving the support they need to succeed.

One of the key components of AI in education is machine learning, a subset of AI that focuses on the development of systems that can learn from data. Machine learning algorithms improve their performance as they are exposed to more information. For instance, an AI-driven educational app might adapt its quizzes based on a child's previous answers, providing more challenging questions when they demonstrate proficiency or offer additional support when they struggle. This level of customization can significantly enhance a child's learning journey, making it more relevant and engaging.

Natural language processing (NLP) is another essential aspect of AI that plays a vital role in educational tools. NLP allows machines to understand and interpret human language, enabling interactive learning experiences. Children can engage with AI tutors through spoken or written language, receiving instant feedback and assistance. This interaction not only makes learning more accessible but also fosters communication skills as children articulate their thoughts and questions in a supportive environment.

As parents navigate the landscape of AI-powered educational tools, understanding these fundamental concepts is crucial. By familiarizing themselves with how AI works and its potential benefits, parents can make informed decisions about the tools their children use. Embracing AI in education opens up new opportunities for personalized learning, allowing children to explore subjects at their own pace while receiving the guidance they need to thrive. As AI continues to evolve, its integration into everyday learning will undoubtedly reshape the educational experiences of future generations.

Chapter 1: Understanding AI in Education

How AI is Changing Learning

The integration of artificial intelligence in education is transforming the traditional learning landscape, offering innovative tools that cater to the diverse needs of children. AI-powered educational tools are designed to adapt to individual learning styles and paces, ensuring that each child receives personalized attention. This adaptive learning approach helps identify strengths and weaknesses, allowing educators and parents to tailor instructional strategies that promote better understanding and retention of information. By leveraging data analytics, these tools can provide insights into a child's learning journey, enabling timely interventions that support their academic growth.

One of the most significant advantages of AI in learning is the accessibility it provides. Children can now engage with educational content anytime and anywhere, breaking down geographical and socioeconomic barriers. AI platforms often include interactive features, gamified learning experiences, and multimedia resources that make learning more engaging and enjoyable. This flexibility not only helps in accommodating different learning environments but also empowers children to take ownership of their education. Parents can support this autonomy by encouraging their children to explore AI tools that resonate with their interests and learning preferences.

Moreover, AI facilitates real-time feedback, which is crucial for effective learning. Unlike traditional assessment methods that may delay results, AI-driven tools can analyze a child's performance instantly, offering constructive feedback that helps reinforce concepts. This immediacy ensures that misconceptions are addressed promptly, fostering a growth mindset. Parents can utilize this feedback to engage in meaningful discussions with their children about their progress, reinforcing the importance of learning from mistakes and celebrating achievements, no matter how small.

In addition to personalized learning experiences, AI can also promote collaboration among students. AI educational platforms include features that allow children to work together on projects or problem-solving tasks, fostering teamwork and communication skills. Such collaborative learning experiences are vital in developing social skills and preparing children for future work environments. Parents can encourage their children to participate in these collaborative activities, helping them to build relationships and learn from their peers while leveraging the benefits of technology.

As AI continues to evolve, it will undoubtedly play an even more significant role in education. Parents must stay informed about the latest developments in AI-powered learning tools and actively engage with their children in this new educational landscape. By understanding how these technologies work and their potential benefits, parents can make informed choices that enhance their children's learning experiences. Embracing AI in education not only supports academic success but also prepares children for a future where technology and learning are intricately intertwined.

The Role of Parents in AI Education

The involvement of parents in their children's education has always been pivotal, and as artificial intelligence (AI) becomes increasingly integrated into educational tools, this role is evolving. Parents are not merely passive observers but active participants in navigating the complexities of AI-powered learning resources. Understanding how to effectively use these tools can enhance a child's educational experience, promote engagement, and foster a cheerful outlook towards learning. By familiarizing themselves with AI technologies, parents can better guide their children in utilizing these resources to their advantage.

One of the primary responsibilities of parents in AI education is to stay informed about the various tools available and their functionalities. This includes understanding how AI can personalize learning experiences, adapt to a child's unique learning pace, and provide instant feedback. Parents should explore educational platforms that leverage AI to create tailored lessons, assess comprehension, and suggest resources that align with their child's learning style. By knowing what tools are out there, parents can make informed decisions about which ones will best support their children's educational needs.

Moreover, parents play a crucial role in setting expectations and boundaries around the use of AI tools. Establishing guidelines for screen time, encouraging breaks, and promoting a balanced approach to technology use can help children reap the benefits while avoiding potential pitfalls. Parents should aim to create an environment where technology serves as a supplement to traditional learning rather than a replacement. This balance can help children develop critical thinking and critical thinking skills, as they learn to navigate both digital and physical learning landscapes.

Engagement between parents and children during the learning process is vital. By actively participating in their child's interaction with AI educational tools, parents can foster a collaborative learning atmosphere. This can involve discussing what the child is learning, asking questions about the material, or even exploring the tools together. Such involvement not only strengthens the parent-child bond but also encourages children to articulate their thoughts and understand the content more deeply. This dialogue can help parents assess their child's progress and adapt their support accordingly.

Lastly, parents must advocate for ethical and responsible use of AI in education. As AI tools continue to evolve, concerns about data privacy and the implications of machine learning on children's development arise. Parents should educate themselves about these issues and instill a sense of responsibility in their children regarding technology use. By discussing topics like digital citizenship and the importance of protecting personal information, parents can help their children navigate the digital world safely and ethically. This initiative-taking approach will empower children to become not just consumers of AI technology but also informed and responsible users.

"It's going to be interesting to see how society deals with artificial intelligence, but it will definitely be cool."

Colin Angle

Chapter 2: Choosing the Right AI Tools

Evaluating Educational Apps

Evaluating educational apps for children requires a thoughtful approach that considers multiple factors, including educational value, user engagement, and developmental appropriateness. Parents should first examine the curriculum alignment of the app. Apps are designed to meet specific educational standards, which can help ensure that the content is relevant and beneficial for your child's learning. Look for apps that are developed in collaboration with educators and experts in child development, as these are more likely to provide quality content that aligns with your child's learning needs.

User engagement is another critical aspect to consider when evaluating educational apps. An effective app should be interactive and engaging, capturing your child's interest while promoting active learning. Pay attention to the app's design and functionality; it should be intuitive and easy to navigate for your child's age group. Look for apps that incorporate gamification elements, such as rewards or challenges, as these can motivate children to return to the app regularly and reinforce learning through play.

Developmental appropriateness is essential when selecting an educational app. Each child is unique, and their learning needs will vary based on age, cognitive development, and personal interests. Parents should assess whether the app offers a variety of difficulty levels or adaptive learning paths that can cater to different skill levels. An app that allows for personalized learning experiences can help children to progress at their own pace, thus fostering a sense of independence and confidence in their abilities.

Another principal factor to consider is the feedback and assessment mechanisms within the app. Quality educational apps provide immediate feedback to children, helping them understand their mistakes and learn from them. Additionally, some apps include progress tracking features that allow parents to monitor their child's development over time. This data can be invaluable for parents seeking to support their child's learning journey and identify areas where additional focus may be needed.

Finally, parents should also consider the app's data privacy and security measures. Many educational apps collect user data, so it is crucial to ensure that the app complies with privacy regulations and prioritizes the safety of your child's information. Look for apps that provide clear explanations of their data usage policies and offer parental controls to manage your child's access. By being vigilant about these factors, parents can make informed choices that enhance their child's learning experience while navigating the increasingly complex world of AI-powered educational tools.

Platforms for Personalized Learning

As the landscape of education continues to evolve, personalized learning platforms have emerged as powerful tools that cater to the unique needs of each child. These platforms utilize artificial intelligence to assess individual learning styles, preferences, and pacing, allowing for a customized educational experience that traditional methods often lack.

Parents are now faced with a plethora of options, making it essential to navigate these tools with a clear understanding of their functionalities and benefits. By leveraging these AI-powered platforms, parents can significantly enhance their child's learning journey.

One of the primary advantages of personalized learning platforms is their ability to adapt content in real-time. As children engage with lessons, these platforms analyze their responses and adjust the difficulty level accordingly. For instance, if a child struggles with a specific math concept, the platform can provide additional resources, practice problems, or even alternative explanations to reinforce understanding. This immediate feedback loop not only aids in comprehension but also fosters a growth mindset, encouraging children to persevere through challenges while feeling supported in their learning.

Additionally, personalized learning platforms often feature a variety of multimedia resources that cater to different learning styles. Visual learners can benefit from videos and interactive simulations, while auditory learners might thrive with podcasts and audio lessons.

Kinesthetic learners, who grasp concepts through movement and firsthand activities, can find engaging tasks that match their needs. By offering a diverse range of materials, these platforms ensure that every child has the opportunity to engage with content in a way that resonates with them, promoting deeper understanding and retention.

Moreover, personalized learning platforms provide parents with valuable insights into their child's progress. Many platforms include dashboards that track performance metrics, allowing parents to monitor strengths and areas for improvement easily. This transparency not only helps parents stay informed but also encourages open dialogue about learning experiences. By discussing the data together, parents can collaborate with their children to set achievable goals, celebrate milestones, and strategize on overcoming obstacles, thus reinforcing the importance of a supportive learning environment at home.

In conclusion, personalized learning platforms represent a significant advancement in educational technology, offering tailored experiences that can greatly benefit children. By understanding the capabilities and features of these tools, parents can make informed decisions that align with their child's learning needs. As AI continues to shape the future of education, embracing these platforms will empower parents to cultivate a more engaging, effective, and personalized learning journey for their children, ultimately transforming the way they experience education at home.

Safety and Privacy Considerations

As parents increasingly adopt AI-powered educational tools for their children, understanding safety and privacy considerations becomes paramount. The integration of artificial intelligence in educational settings brings numerous benefits, such as personalized learning experiences and adaptive content delivery. However, these advantages must be balanced against potential risks to children's safety and privacy. Parents should be well-informed about these considerations to make educated choices regarding the tools they integrate into their children's learning environments.

One of the primary safety concerns associated with AI tools is the risk of exposure to inappropriate content. Many educational platforms utilize algorithms to curate content for children, but there is always a possibility of errors in content filtering. Parents should investigate the mechanisms that each tool employs to ensure age-appropriate material. Additionally, regular monitoring of the content accessed by children can help mitigate the risk of exposure to harmful or unsuitable information, allowing for a safer learning experience.

Privacy is another critical aspect that parents need to address when selecting AI-powered educational tools. These platforms often collect data on user interactions to enhance personalization and improve educational outcomes. Parents should carefully review privacy policies to understand what data is collected, how it is used, and whether it is shared with third parties. Transparency in data handling practices is essential, as is the ability for parents to control or delete their child's data when necessary.

Furthermore, parents should be aware of the age restrictions and consent requirements associated with various educational tools. Many platforms are designed with specific age groups in mind, and compliance with regulations such as the Children's Online Privacy Protection Act (COPPA) is crucial. These regulations are intended to protect children's online experiences, ensuring that their information is safeguarded. By choosing platforms that adhere to these standards, parents can help create a secure digital learning environment for their children.

Finally, fostering open communication about safety and privacy with children is vital. Educating children about the importance of protecting their personal information can empower them to navigate digital spaces more responsibly. Encouraging discussions about online safety, including recognizing suspicious activities and understanding the implications of sharing personal information, will help children become more aware and cautious users of AI-powered educational tools. By taking these proactive steps, parents can enhance the overall learning experience while safeguarding their children's well-being in an increasingly digital educational landscape.

Fun and Educational AI Tools for Kids to Use at Home

Artificial Intelligence (AI) is transforming the way children learn, play, and explore innovative ideas. With the right guidance, AI-powered tools can help kids develop creativity, problem-solving skills, and even improve their academic performance. However, parental supervision is essential to ensure safe and productive use.

Here are some kid-friendly AI tools that can be used at home under parental guidance:

1. AI-Powered Learning Assistants

a. Khan Academy Kids (Ages 2-8)

What it does: Offers interactive lessons in math, reading, and social-emotional learning.
AI Feature: Adapts to the child's learning pace.
Parental Role: Parents can track progress and set learning goals.

b. Duolingo ABC (Ages 3-6)

What it does: Helps young kids learn reading and writing through gamified lessons.
AI Feature: Adjusts difficulty based on performance.
Parental Role: Parents can monitor progress and encourage daily practice.

c. Socratic by Google (Ages 10+)

What it does: Helps with homework by answering questions via AI (math, science, history).
AI Feature: Uses image recognition to solve problems.
Parental Role: Supervise usage to ensure kids try solving problems first before relying on AI.

2. Creative AI Tools for Kids

a. Canva for Kids (Ages 6+)

What it does: A simplified version of Canva where kids can design posters, cards, and simple animations.
AI Feature: AI-powered design suggestions.
Parental Role: Help kids navigate the tool and encourage creative projects.

b. DALL·E Mini (Ages 8+ with supervision)

What it does: Generates fun images based on text prompts (e.g., "a cat wearing a superhero cape").
AI Feature: Uses AI to create unique artwork.
Parental Role: Monitor prompts to ensure appropriate content.

c. Boomy (Ages 10+)

What it does: Lets kids create their own music using AI.
AI Feature: Generates beats and melodies based on preferences.
Parental Role: Assist in exploring music creation safely.

3. AI Coding & Robotics for Kids

a. Scratch (Ages 5+)

What it does: A block-based coding platform developed by MIT.
AI Feature: Some extensions allow AI integration (e.g., speech recognition).
Parental Role: Help kids understand basic coding concepts.

b. Cognimates (Ages 7+)

What it does: AI-powered platform where kids can train their own AI models, code games, and interact with robots.

AI Feature: Teaches machine learning basics in a kid-friendly way.

Parental Role: Guide kids through AI experiments.

c. LEGO Mindstorms (Ages 9+)

What it does: Combines LEGO robotics with simple AI programming.

AI Feature: Kids can program robots to respond to voice or movement.

Parental Role: Assist in building and coding projects.

4. AI Storytelling & Writing Helpers

a. Storybird (Ages 6+)

What it does: Helps kids write and illustrate stories with AI-generated prompts.

AI Feature: Suggests story ideas and artwork.

Parental Role: Encourage storytelling and review content.

b. ChatGPT (Ages 10+ with supervision)

What it does: Helps kids brainstorm stories, explain concepts, or practice writing.
AI Feature: Conversational AI that responds to prompts.
Parental Role: Monitor interactions to ensure appropriate use.

Safety Tips for Parents Using AI with Kids:

✓ Supervise usage – Always check what kids are doing with AI tools.
✓ Set time limits – Balance screen time with offline activities.
✓ Encourage creativity – Use AI as a tool, not a replacement for thinking.
✓ Check privacy policies – Ensure the tool is COPPA-compliant (child-safe).

Final Thoughts

AI can be a fantastic educational and creative tool for kids when used responsibly. By exploring these AI-powered platforms together, parents can help their children learn, create, and innovate in a fun and safe way.

Note: Always review AI tools before introducing them to kids, as some may have age restrictions or require accounts. Parental involvement ensures a positive and secure experience.

Chapter 3: Integrating AI into Daily Learning

Setting Up a Learning Environment

Creating a conducive learning environment is essential for maximizing the benefits of AI-powered educational tools for children. The first step in setting up this environment is to designate a specific area in your home that is quiet, well-lit, and free from distractions. This space should be comfortable and equipped with necessary supplies such as notebooks, writing instruments, and access to a computer or tablet. Ensuring that this area is organized and inviting can significantly enhance your child's focus and motivation to engage with their learning materials.

Equipping the learning space with the right technology is crucial. Ensure that the devices used are compatible with the educational tools your child will be utilizing. This includes installing necessary software and applications that enhance learning experiences, such as interactive platforms or AI-driven tutoring systems. Additionally, maintaining a stable internet connection is vital for uninterrupted access to these resources. By investing in reliable technology, you set the groundwork for your child to explore and learn effectively.

Incorporating a routine into the learning environment can further improve your child's educational experience. Establishing specific times for learning activities helps to create a structured approach, which is beneficial for many children. This routine can include breaks to prevent burnout and time allocated for different subjects or activities, allowing the use of various AI tools to diversify learning. By being consistent with this schedule, children can develop a powerful sense of responsibility and commitment to their education.

Parental involvement plays a significant role in optimizing the learning environment. Actively engaging with your child during their learning sessions can help you gauge their understanding and interests. Encouraging discussions about the educational tools they are using can also foster a deeper connection to the material. By showing genuine interest and providing support, you can boost your child's confidence and enthusiasm for learning, making the experience more enjoyable and effective.

Finally, fostering a growth mindset is essential for navigating the challenges that may arise while using AI-powered educational tools. Encourage your child to view mistakes as opportunities for learning rather than setbacks. Celebrating their achievements, no matter how small, can boost motivation and resilience. By instilling a positive attitude towards learning, you help your child develop the skills necessary to adapt to innovative technologies and educational methodologies, ultimately enhancing their overall learning experience.

Establishing a Routine with AI Tools

Establishing a routine with AI tools can create a structured learning environment that benefits children's educational experiences. By integrating these tools into daily activities, parents can enhance their children's engagement and motivation. A well-defined routine helps children understand expectations and fosters a sense of security, which is essential for effective learning. Incorporating AI-powered educational tools into this routine can support personalized learning, making it easier for children to grasp complex concepts and develop critical skills.

To begin, parents should assess their children's individual learning styles and preferences. This understanding will guide the selection of appropriate AI tools that align with their educational needs. For instance, some children may thrive with interactive learning platforms that gamify education, while others may prefer more structured programs that focus on skill mastery. By identifying these preferences, parents can create a tailored routine that incorporates specific AI tools, ensuring that learning remains engaging and relevant to each child.

Once the appropriate tools are selected, establishing a consistent schedule is crucial. This schedule should include designated times for using AI tools, interspersed with breaks and other activities to prevent burnout. Consistency reinforces the importance of education and helps children develop self-discipline. Parents can collaborate with their children to set realistic goals for each session, ensuring that the time spent using AI tools is productive and aligned with their overall learning objectives.

Encouraging parental involvement in the routine can further enhance the effectiveness of AI tools. Parents can participate in learning sessions, provide guidance, and engage in discussions about the material being covered. This involvement not only reinforces the child's learning but also strengthens the parent-child bond. Additionally, parents can monitor progress through the analytics often provided by AI tools, allowing them to address any challenges promptly and adjust the routine as necessary to meet their child's evolving needs.

Finally, flexibility is essential when establishing a routine with AI tools. While consistency is important, parents should remain open to adapting the schedule based on their child's interests and feedback. This adaptability can help maintain enthusiasm for learning and allow for the incorporation of new educational tools as they become available. By fostering a dynamic and responsive learning environment, parents can maximize the benefits of AI-powered educational tools, ultimately transforming their child's learning experience at home.

Encouraging Independent Learning

Encouraging independent learning in children is a vital aspect of their educational journey, particularly in an age where technology offers unprecedented access to information and resources. Parents play a crucial role in fostering this independence by creating an environment that promotes exploration and self-directed study. One effective approach is to introduce AI-powered educational tools that adapt to a child's learning style and pace. These tools can provide personalized learning experiences, enabling children to take charge of their education and develop critical thinking skills.

To nurture independent learning, parents should first assess their child's interests and strengths. By understanding what captivates their child's attention, parents can select AI-based platforms and resources that align with these interests. For example, if a child is fascinated by science, parents can introduce them to interactive AI programs that offer experiments or simulations. This tailored approach not only enhances engagement but also encourages children to seek knowledge proactively, fostering a sense of ownership over their learning.

Moreover, establishing a routine that includes designated study times can significantly enhance independent learning. Parents can encourage their children to set goals for each session, whether it is completing a specific module on an educational app or exploring a new concept. By guiding children to plan their learning activities, parents help them develop time management skills and the ability to prioritize tasks. This structure, combined with the flexibility of AI tools, allows children to pursue their interests while learning to manage their responsibilities.

Encouraging reflection is another essential component of independent learning. After engaging with AI educational tools, parents can prompt their children to discuss what they learned, what challenges they faced, and how they overcame them. This practice not only reinforces the knowledge gained but also cultivates metacognitive skills, helping children become more aware of their learning processes.

By fostering a culture of reflection, parents empower their children to evaluate their progress and adapt their strategies for future learning endeavors.

Finally, parents should celebrate successes, both big and small, to motivate their children in their independent learning journey. Acknowledging achievements, whether through verbal praise or small rewards, reinforces positive behavior and encourages continued exploration. As children gain confidence in their abilities, they are more likely to embrace challenges and seek out new learning opportunities. By supporting their child's independent learning with the right tools and encouragement, parents can help cultivate a lifelong love of learning that will serve them well beyond their formative years.

"Some people worry that artificial intelligence will make us feel inferior, but then, anybody in his right mind should have an inferiority complex every time he looks at a flower."
Alan Kay

Chapter 4: Enhancing Learning with AI

Interactive Learning Experiences

Interactive learning experiences have become increasingly prominent in the landscape of education, particularly with the integration of AI-powered tools. These experiences engage children in ways that traditional methods may not, fostering a deeper understanding of concepts and enhancing retention. By leveraging technology, parents can provide their children with opportunities to explore subjects through interactive simulations, educational games, and personalized learning platforms that adapt to their unique learning styles and paces.

One significant advantage of AI-driven educational tools is their ability to create personalized learning experiences. These tools can assess a child's strengths and weaknesses in real time, adjusting the content accordingly. For example, AI can identify specific areas where a child struggles with math concepts and offer targeted exercises or alternative explanations that resonate with their understanding. This individualized approach not only builds confidence but also motivates children to engage more actively with their studies.

Interactive learning experiences also promote collaboration and communication among peers. Many AI-based platforms incorporate features that enable children to work together on projects or challenges, even when they are not physically in the same location. This collaborative environment nurtures essential social skills such as teamwork, problem-solving, and critical thinking. Parents can encourage their children to participate in these interactive settings, reinforcing the idea that learning can be a communal and enjoyable endeavor.

Moreover, the incorporation of gamification in educational tools enhances motivation and engagement. By turning lessons into games, children are more likely to immerse themselves in the learning process. Points, badges, and rewards can create a sense of achievement, making the educational journey feel less like a chore and more like an adventure. Parents should look for platforms that utilize gamification effectively, as it can significantly boost their child's desire to learn and explore new subjects.

Finally, interactive learning experiences often extend beyond the screen. AI-powered tools encourage firsthand activities that reinforce digital lessons, bridging the gap between virtual and physical learning. For instance, a science app might prompt children to conduct simple experiments at home, allowing them to see real-world applications of their studies. By supporting these interactive experiences, parents can help cultivate a love for learning that will last a lifetime, equipping their children with the skills they need to thrive in an increasingly technology-driven world.

Using AI for Homework Help

Using AI for homework help has become an increasingly popular method for parents seeking to enhance their children's learning experience. As educational technology continues to advance, AI-powered tools offer personalized assistance that can cater to individual learning styles and needs. These applications can provide explanations, examples, and practice problems, helping students grasp complex concepts more effectively. Parents can leverage these tools to support their children's homework routines, ensuring that they understand the material and gain confidence in their abilities.

One of the most significant advantages of using AI for homework assistance is the accessibility it provides. With a variety of platforms available, students can access help anytime and anywhere, breaking the limitations of traditional tutoring sessions. AI tools can analyze a child's progress, identify areas of difficulty, and offer tailored resources to address those challenges. This immediate feedback loop is invaluable, as it allows students to work at their own pace while receiving the support they need to succeed in their studies.

Moreover, AI-powered homework help can encourage independent learning. As students engage with these tools, they develop critical thinking and critical thinking skills by navigating challenges on their own. This fosters a sense of ownership over their education, empowering them to seek answers and explore subjects beyond the confines of their curriculum. Parents can facilitate this journey by introducing their children to reliable AI resources and encouraging them to utilize these tools as a supplement to traditional learning methods.

While integrating AI into homework help can yield numerous benefits, it is essential for parents to remain actively involved in their children's learning process. Monitoring the use of these tools ensures that students are not solely relying on AI for answers but are instead engaging with the material in a meaningful way. Parents can discuss homework assignments with their children, encouraging them to think critically about the information provided by AI tools. This dialogue not only reinforces learning but also strengthens the parent-child relationship as they collaborate on educational challenges.

In conclusion, AI for homework help represents a transformative opportunity for enhancing children's educational experiences. By utilizing AI-powered tools, parents can provide their children with the resources they need to thrive academically. However, it is crucial to balance technology use with active parental involvement to foster a well-rounded approach to learning. Embracing AI as a supportive educational partner can help children develop the skills necessary to succeed in an increasingly digital world while ensuring that they remain engaged and curious learners.

Gamification and Learning

Gamification is a powerful strategy that leverages game design elements to enhance educational experiences. In the context of AI-powered learning tools, gamification can engage children in ways that traditional teaching methods often cannot. By incorporating elements such as points, levels, and rewards, these tools create an interactive environment that motivates children to participate actively in their learning journey. This approach not only makes education enjoyable but also encourages children to embrace challenges and develop a growth mindset.

Children are naturally drawn to games, which makes gamification an effective method for capturing their attention. When educational content is presented in a game-like format, it resonates with children's inherent desire for play and exploration. AI-powered educational tools can personalize the learning experience by adapting to each child's unique preferences and learning pace. This tailored approach ensures that children remain engaged and motivated, as they progress through challenges suited to their individual skill levels.

Moreover, gamification fosters essential skills such as critical thinking, problem-solving, and collaboration. Many gamified learning platforms incorporate multiplayer features, allowing children to work together to solve problems or complete tasks. This collaborative aspect not only enhances social skills but also teaches children the importance of teamwork and communication. As they navigate through challenges, they learn to strategize, negotiate, and support one another, skills that are increasingly vital in today's interconnected world.

The immediate feedback provided by gamified systems is another significant advantage. In traditional educational settings, children often receive feedback only after completing assignments or tests. However, AI-powered gamified tools offer real-time responses that help children understand their mistakes and learn from them instantly. This immediate reinforcement aids in retaining knowledge and encourages a continuous cycle of learning and improvement. As children receive rewards for their accomplishments, they experience a sense of achievement that further drives their motivation.

While gamification presents numerous benefits, it is essential for parents to guide their children in navigating these tools effectively. Setting limits on screen time, encouraging breaks, and fostering discussions about what they learn can help ensure that the gaming experience remains educational. Parents should also take an active role in selecting appropriate gamified tools that align with their child's educational goals. By actively engaging in their child's learning process and understanding the role of gamification, parents can help create a balanced and enriching educational environment that leverages the power of AI.

"AI is the new electricity."
Andrew Ng

Chapter 5: Supporting Diverse Learning Needs

AI for Different Learning Styles

Artificial Intelligence (AI) has the potential to revolutionize how children learn by accommodating various learning styles. Understanding that each child has a unique way of processing information is crucial for parents seeking to enhance their educational experience. AI-powered tools can analyze a child's learning habits, preferences, and challenges, allowing for personalized educational approaches that cater to visual, auditory, reading/writing, and kinesthetic learners. By leveraging these technologies, parents can ensure their children receive tailored support that aligns with their individual needs.

For visual learners, AI tools can provide interactive and visually stimulating content that aids in comprehension. Programs that incorporate graphics, videos, and infographics can help these children grasp complex concepts more easily. For example, AI-driven platforms can generate personalized visual aids based on a child's curriculum, turning abstract ideas into concrete images that resonate with their learning style. Parents can seek out educational apps that emphasize visual storytelling and graphic representations, making learning more engaging and effective for their visually oriented children.

Auditory learners thrive on listening and verbal interaction. AI can enhance their learning experience by offering features such as voice-assisted technology and interactive audio lessons. These tools can read aloud text, provide spoken explanations, and even engage in conversational practice, all of which can help auditory learners absorb information more thoroughly. Parents can explore AI applications that focus on language acquisition and storytelling, where children can listen to narratives and engage in discussions, reinforcing their understanding through auditory means.

For those who excel in reading and writing, AI can assist by providing tools that adapt to their literacy skills. AI-driven educational software can suggest reading materials and writing prompts that are tailored to a child's proficiency level, encouraging them to explore literature at their own pace. Additionally, some platforms are equipped with grammar and style checkers that provide real-time feedback, helping young writers refine their skills. Parents can guide their children toward AI resources that cultivate a love for reading and writing, ensuring they have the necessary tools to express themselves effectively.

Kinesthetic learners require direct experience to fully engage with educational content. AI technology can cater to these learners by integrating gamification and interactive simulations into their learning processes. Educational games powered by AI can provide real-world challenges that encourage problem-solving and critical thinking, allowing kinesthetic learners to apply their knowledge in practical scenarios. Parents should seek out AI-enhanced tools that promote active participation, ensuring that their children can learn through movement and exploration, which aligns with their natural learning preferences.

Addressing Special Educational Needs

Addressing special educational needs is a critical aspect of leveraging AI-powered educational tools to enhance the learning experience for all children, particularly those who require additional support. As parents, understanding how these tools can be tailored to meet the unique needs of your child is essential. AI technology can offer personalized learning experiences that adapt to individual learning styles, pace, and specific challenges, ensuring that every child can benefit from the educational opportunities available.

AI tools can be incredibly effective in identifying and addressing the specific needs of children with learning difficulties. These platforms often utilize data-driven assessments to evaluate a child's strengths and weaknesses, allowing for a customized learning plan that targets areas requiring additional attention. For instance, children with dyslexia may benefit from AI-driven reading apps that incorporate phonetic awareness exercises, while those with attention difficulties might thrive in environments that use gamification to maintain engagement.

Moreover, the adaptability of AI tools extends beyond academic content. Many apps have features that help children with disabilities. Voice recognition technology, for example, can assist children who struggle with writing by allowing them to dictate their thoughts and ideas. Similarly, visual aids and interactive simulations can help students with sensory processing issues engage more fully with the material, making learning a more inclusive experience.

Parental involvement remains crucial in this process. As parents, you have the opportunity to collaborate with educators and AI tool developers to ensure that the technology being used aligns with your child's specific needs. Regular communication with teachers can provide insights into your child's progress and the effectiveness of the tools being employed. Additionally, participating in workshops or forums focused on special educational needs can equip you with the knowledge necessary to advocate for your child and make informed decisions regarding the use of AI tools.

In conclusion, addressing special educational needs through AI-powered educational tools requires a multifaceted approach that combines technology, parental involvement, and collaboration with educators. By embracing these tools and understanding how they can be tailored to your child's unique learning journey, you can play a pivotal role in transforming their educational experience. This initiative-taking engagement not only empowers your child but also fosters a supportive learning environment that values diversity and inclusiveness in education.

Language Learning with AI

Language learning has traditionally been a labor-intensive process, often requiring considerable time and effort from both students and educators. However, the advent of artificial intelligence (AI) has revolutionized this landscape, offering innovative tools that make language acquisition more efficient and engaging for children. AI-powered language learning applications now provide personalized experiences that adapt to individual learning styles, helping children overcome challenges and build confidence in their language skills.

One of the key advantages of using AI in language learning is its ability to customize the learning experience based on a child's proficiency level and learning pace. Innumerable AI-driven platforms employ sophisticated algorithms to assess a learner's strengths and weaknesses, curating lessons that target specific areas for improvement. This tailored approach ensures that children remain engaged and motivated, as they can progress through levels that match their abilities, rather than being held back or pushed too quickly through a one-size-fits-all curriculum.

Moreover, AI language learning tools often incorporate interactive elements that make the process enjoyable. Features such as gamification, where language exercises are presented as games or challenges, encourage children to practice more frequently and with greater enthusiasm. Additionally, these platforms often include voice recognition technology, allowing children to practice pronunciation and receive immediate feedback. This immediate reinforcement is critical for language acquisition, as it helps children correct mistakes in real-time and develop their speaking skills more effectively.

Parental involvement is essential in maximizing the benefits of AI-powered language learning tools. Parents can take an active role by monitoring their child's progress through the application's analytics, which often provide insights into performance and areas needing attention. Engaging with children during their language practice sessions can also enhance the learning experience. Parents can encourage discussions about the new vocabulary or grammar rules learned, fostering a supportive environment that reinforces language use in everyday contexts.

As AI continues to advance, the potential for its application in language learning will only grow. Emerging technologies such as augmented reality and immersive environments may soon offer even more dynamic ways for children to practice languages in contextually rich scenarios. By embracing these AI-powered tools, parents can help their children not only learn a new language but also develop a lifelong love for learning and exploration. The integration of AI in language education represents a significant step forward, paving the way for a future where language barriers are diminished, and global communication is more accessible than ever.

> *"The question of whether machines can think is about as relevant as the question of whether submarines can swim."*
> **Edsger Dijkstra**

Chapter 6: Monitoring Progress and Engagement

Tracking Learning Outcomes

Tracking learning outcomes is essential for understanding how effectively your child is engaging with AI-powered educational tools. These tools often provide a wealth of data that can help parents gauge their child's progress in various subjects. By monitoring these outcomes, you can identify areas where your child excels and where they may need additional support. This data-driven approach allows for more informed conversations with educators and can guide your child's learning journey more effectively.

One of the key features of AI educational platforms is their ability to customize learning experiences based on individual performance. These platforms typically offer assessments that can pinpoint a child's strengths and weaknesses. For instance, if your child struggles with math concepts, the AI can adjust the curriculum to provide more targeted exercises and resources. By regularly reviewing these assessments, parents can track improvements over time and celebrate achievements, fostering motivation and a cheerful outlook towards learning.

In addition to formal assessments, AI tools incorporate gamification elements, which can also serve as indicators of learning outcomes. By observing your child's engagement with these elements, you can gauge their interest in specific topics. High engagement levels often correlate with better understanding and retention of information. Parents should take the time to discuss these experiences with their children, allowing them to articulate what they enjoy and what challenges they face, thereby enhancing the learning process.

It is crucial to set specific goals based on the insights gained from tracking learning outcomes. For instance, if your child has been working on reading comprehension, you might aim for them to complete a certain number of books or achieve a specific score on a reading assessment within a set period. These goals provide clarity and a sense of direction in your child's learning journey. Furthermore, they enable parents to provide targeted encouragement and resources, reinforcing the idea that learning is a collaborative effort.

Finally, maintaining an open line of communication with your child's teachers and educators is vital when tracking learning outcomes. AI tools can provide valuable insights, but they are most effective when integrated with traditional educational methods. Regular updates from teachers can help contextualize the data and offer additional strategies for supporting your child's learning at home. By working together, parents and educators can create a cohesive support system that maximizes the benefits of AI-powered educational tools and enhances your child's overall learning experience.

Encouraging Feedback and Communication

Encouraging feedback and communication is essential for maximizing the benefits of AI-powered educational tools in your child's learning experience. As parents, fostering an environment where open dialogue about these tools can thrive not only enhances their educational journey but also helps you understand their needs and preferences. Regular discussions can illuminate how your child interacts with AI-driven platforms, ensuring that you remain engaged and supportive in their learning process.

One effective approach is to establish a routine for discussing your child's experiences with AI tools. This could be a weekly check-in where you ask open-ended questions about what they learned, what they enjoyed, and any challenges they faced. Encouraging your child to articulate their thoughts promotes critical thinking and self-reflection, key components of a successful learning experience. By actively listening to their feedback, you not only validate their feelings but also gain valuable insights into how the tools are impacting their education.

Another critical aspect of encouraging feedback is modeling effective communication skills. Demonstrate how to provide constructive feedback by sharing your observations about their use of AI tools. For instance, if your child struggled with a specific concept, discuss ways to approach it differently. This creates a safe space for them to express their difficulties and successes, reinforcing the idea that feedback is a valuable part of the learning process. As they see you engage in constructive dialogue, they are more likely to mirror these behaviors in their interactions with both you and technology.

In addition to direct conversations, consider leveraging technology to facilitate feedback. AI educational tools provide built-in features for tracking progress and providing reports. Encourage your child to share these insights with you, discussing what they mean and how they can guide future learning. This not only helps you stay informed about your child's development but also empowers your child to take ownership of their learning. Understanding their progress through data can motivate them and encourage an initiative-taking approach to their education.

Finally, fostering a culture of feedback extends beyond the parent-child dynamic. Encourage your child to communicate with their teachers or mentors about their experiences with AI tools. This can lead to a collaborative approach to learning, where educators can adjust their methods based on student feedback. By promoting open lines of communication, you help create a more responsive and personalized learning environment, ensuring that AI-powered educational tools serve as effective aids in your child's academic journey.

Adjusting Tools Based on Performance

Adjusting tools based on performance is essential for maximizing the benefits of AI-powered educational resources in your child's learning journey. As parents, it is important to recognize that not all tools will yield the same results for every child. Children possess unique learning styles, preferences, and paces, which can significantly influence how they engage with educational technologies. By monitoring your child's performance and engagement levels, you can make informed decisions about which tools to continue using, which ones need adjustment, and which may need to be replaced altogether.

One effective strategy for adjusting educational tools involves regularly assessing your child's progress. AI-powered platforms are equipped with analytics that track learning outcomes, engagement metrics, and even emotional responses to various tasks. By reviewing these insights, you can identify areas where your child excels and where they may be struggling. For instance, if a particular math application shows that your child is consistently scoring low on problem-solving modules, it may be time to explore additional resources or modify the existing tool to better suit their needs.

Feedback from your child is another critical component of adjusting tools based on performance. Engaging in open conversations about their experiences with different educational technologies can provide valuable insights. Ask questions about what they enjoy, what frustrates them, and how they feel about their learning progress. This feedback not only empowers your child but also helps you tailor the educational tools to align with their interests and motivations. If your child is disengaged with a reading app, for example, it might be worth considering alternative platforms or incorporating more interactive features to reignite their interest.

Moreover, flexibility is key when it comes to adapting educational tools. As your child's learning needs evolve, so should the resources you provide too. This might mean transitioning to more advanced platforms as they gain skills or opting for tools that focus on different subjects to provide a well-rounded educational experience. Staying informed about the latest innovations in AI-powered education can also guide your decisions, ensuring that you are utilizing the most effective tools available. Continuous exploration and willingness to adapt can enhance your child's learning experience significantly.

Finally, collaboration with educators can enhance your ability to adjust tools based on performance. Teachers often have insights into effective strategies and resources that align with curriculum standards and your child's needs. By communicating with your child's educators, you can gain recommendations for supplementary tools or adjustments to existing ones, ensuring a cohesive approach to learning both at home and in the classroom. This collaboration helps create a supportive learning environment that promotes your child's academic growth and confidence, ultimately transforming their educational experience through the effective use of AI technology.

Chapter 7: Creating a Balanced Approach

Limiting Screen Time

Limiting screen time is an essential aspect of fostering a healthy learning environment for children, especially in an age where AI-powered educational tools are increasingly integrated into daily life. While these tools offer significant educational benefits, it is crucial for parents to establish guidelines that prevent excessive screen exposure. Research indicates that prolonged screen time can lead to various developmental issues, including problems with attention, sleep, and social interactions. Therefore, setting boundaries around screen use is not only beneficial but necessary for a balanced approach to learning.

To effectively limit screen time, parents should start by understanding the recommended guidelines for different age groups. The American Academy of Pediatrics suggests that children aged 2 to 5 should have no more than one hour of high-quality programming each day, while children aged 6 and older should have consistent limits on screen time to ensure it does not interfere with sleep, physical activity, and other healthy behaviors. By adhering to these recommendations, parents can create a structured environment that promotes both the use of AI tools for learning and the importance of offline activities.

Incorporating screen time limits into daily routines can be achieved through various strategies. One effective method is to develop a family media plan that outlines when and how screens will be used. This plan should consider educational objectives, leisure time, and family activities. Designating specific times for using AI-powered educational tools, such as homework or study sessions, can help ensure that technology serves its intended purpose without encroaching on family interactions or physical playtime. Additionally, parents can encourage alternative learning methods, such as reading, firsthand projects, or outdoor activities, to complement the use of technology.

Monitoring the content that children consume is equally important when limiting screen time. Parents should engage with their children by discussing the educational tools they use and exploring the material together. This not only reinforces the learning experience but also provides an opportunity to teach critical thinking skills about the information encountered online. By actively participating in their children's digital education, parents can better understand the benefits and potential drawbacks of AI resources, fostering a more balanced approach to technology use.

Finally, it is essential to model healthy screen habits as parents. Children often emulate their parents' behavior, so demonstrating responsible screen use can have a profound impact on their understanding of balance. Prioritizing family time without screens, participating in offline hobbies, and setting personal limits on technology use can serve as powerful examples for children. By working together as a family to establish and respect screen time boundaries, parents can cultivate an environment where AI-powered educational tools enhance learning rather than dominate it.

Combining Traditional Learning with AI

As parents, understanding the potential of combining traditional learning methods with artificial intelligence (AI) can significantly enhance your child's educational experience. Traditional learning has long been the cornerstone of education, focusing on structured curricula, teacher-led instruction, and well-defined learning objectives. However, introducing AI-powered tools into this framework can create a more personalized and adaptive learning environment. This integration allows for tailored educational experiences that cater to your child's unique learning style, pace, and interests, fostering a deeper engagement with the material.

One of the most significant advantages of AI in education is its ability to analyze data and provide real-time feedback. Traditional learning often relies on periodic assessments to gauge student progress, which can sometimes miss the nuances of a child's learning journey. AI tools can continuously monitor performance, identify areas where a child may struggle, and offer immediate interventions. For example, if a child is having difficulty with a particular math concept, AI-driven platforms can provide additional resources, practice problems, or even alternative explanations tailored to that child's understanding. This immediate responsiveness can help reinforce traditional teaching efforts and ensure that no child is left behind.

Moreover, the integration of AI can support traditional learning by enhancing the curriculum with interactive and engaging content. AI educational tools incorporate gamification, personalized quizzes, and multimedia resources that transform standard lessons into captivating learning experiences. For instance, a history lesson might be enriched with interactive timelines or virtual reality experiences that allow children to explore historical events in a more immersive way. By merging these engaging elements with traditional content, children are more likely to retain knowledge and develop a genuine interest in the subjects they are studying.

Collaboration is another area where the fusion of traditional learning and AI can be beneficial. Classrooms often emphasize group work and peer learning, which are essential for developing social skills and teamwork. AI tools can facilitate this by connecting students with similar interests or complementary skills, allowing them to collaborate on projects or study groups regardless of physical location. This not only enhances the learning experience but also prepares children for a future where collaboration across digital platforms is increasingly prevalent. Parents can encourage their children to leverage these tools while still valuing the importance of in-person interactions and teamwork.

Finally, as parents, it is crucial to remain actively involved in your child's educational journey. While AI tools can provide significant support, they should complement, not replace, traditional learning methods. Engaging with your child about their use of AI in education can foster discussions about what they are learning and how they prefer to learn. By maintaining an open dialogue, parents can help their children develop a balanced approach to education that values both traditional methods and innovative technologies. This partnership between parents, children, and AI-powered tools can create a holistic learning environment that prepares children for success in an increasingly digital world.

How to Combine Traditional Learning with AI Tools for Kids at Home

In today's digital age, Artificial Intelligence (AI) is revolutionizing education, offering new ways to enhance learning. However, traditional learning methods—such as reading physical books, handwriting, and hands-on activities—remain essential for cognitive development. The key is finding the right balance between classic educational techniques and cutting-edge AI tools to create a well-rounded learning experience for kids.

Here's how parents can effectively combine traditional learning with AI at home:

1. Reinforce Reading & Writing with AI Assistance

Traditional Method:

📖 Encourage kids to read physical books and practice handwriting.

✍️ Have them draft stories or journal entries by hand.

AI Integration:

Use AI tools like ChatGPT or Storybird to generate creative writing prompts.

Try speech-to-text apps (like Google Docs Voice Typing) to help struggling writers express ideas before writing them down.

Apps like Khan Academy Kids can recommend books based on reading level while still encouraging offline reading.

Parent's Role:

✅ Set a routine—e.g., 30 minutes of reading a physical book, then 15 minutes of AI-assisted writing.

✅ Discuss AI-generated ideas together to enhance comprehension.

2. Enhance Math Skills with AI & Hands-On Practice

Traditional Method:

📊 Use flashcards, abacus, or physical worksheets for arithmetic practice.

📐 Solve real-world math problems (e.g., measuring ingredients while cooking).

AI Integration:

Apps like Photomath scan handwritten problems and explain solutions step-by-step.

Prodigy Math Game adapts difficulty based on the child's level while keeping learning fun.

Coding with Scratch helps kids apply math concepts in interactive projects.

Parent's Role:

✅ Start with traditional methods, then use AI to check answers or explore advanced concepts.

✅ Combine digital and physical learning—e.g., solve problems on paper first, then verify with an AI tool.

3. Blend Science Experiments with AI Exploration

Traditional Method:

🔬 Conduct modest home experiments (volcano eruptions, plant growth tracking).

🌍 Use globes, maps, and encyclopedias for geography and biology.

AI Integration:

Google's Science Journal app records and analyzes experiment data (e.g., measuring light or sound).

AI-powered tools like Cognimates let kids train their own machine-learning models (e.g., identifying plant species).

Virtual lab simulations (e.g., Labster) provide interactive science experiences.

Parent's Role:

✅ Start with a real-world experiment, then use AI to analyze results.

✅ Encourage kids to ask AI questions (e.g., "Why did the baking soda volcano erupt?") and discuss answers together.

4. Combine Art & Creativity with AI Inspiration

Traditional Method:
🎨 Drawing, painting, and crafting with physical materials.

✂️ Building models with clay, LEGO, or recycled materials.

AI Integration:
DALL·E or Canva for Kids generates AI art for inspiration before drawing.

Boomy AI helps compose music, which kids can then play on real instruments.

Stop-motion animation apps (like Stop Motion Studio) bring handmade creations to life.

Parent's Role:
✅ Use AI-generated art as a prompt ("Can you draw your own version of this?").

✅ Encourage kids to mix digital and physical creativity (e.g., design a character with AI, then sculpt it with clay).

5. Develop Critical Thinking with AI & Real-World Discussions

Traditional Method:
🗣️ Family debates, board games, and puzzles.

📰 Reading newspapers or history books together.

AI Integration:

Use ChatGPT (with supervision) to debate topics or simulate historical conversations.

AI quiz apps (like Quizlet) reinforce facts through interactive flashcards.

Coding robots (LEGO Mindstorms) teach logic through hands-on programming.

Parent's Role:

✅ Compare AI answers with real sources—teach kids to fact-check.

✅ Discuss ethical questions: "Should AI do homework for us? Why or why not?"

6. Balance Screen Time with Offline Learning

While AI is powerful, too much screen time can be counterproductive. Here is how to maintain balance:

✔ Set a schedule – e.g., 30 minutes of AI learning, then 30 minutes of reading or hands-on play.

✔ Use AI as a supplement, not a replacement – Encourage kids to solve problems manually first.

✔ Encourage outdoor & social learning – Visit libraries, museums, or science centers to reinforce digital lessons.

Final Thoughts

The best learning happens when traditional methods and AI tools work together. By blending hands-on activities with smart technology, parents can create a dynamic, engaging, and balanced education for their kids.

Key Takeaways:

- Use AI to enhance, not replace, traditional learning.
- Encourage critical thinking by comparing AI answers with real-world knowledge.
- Maintain a healthy balance between digital and offline activities.

Encouraging Physical Activity and Social Interaction

In today's digital age, fostering physical activity and social interaction among children is more crucial than ever. While AI-powered educational tools offer countless benefits in enhancing learning experiences, they can inadvertently contribute to a sedentary lifestyle if not balanced with active pursuits. Parents play a vital role in guiding their children to integrate these tools into a well-rounded daily routine that prioritizes both education and physical well-being. Encouraging a lifestyle that balances screen time with active play can significantly enhance children's overall development.

AI technologies can be utilized to create engaging environments that promote physical activity. For instance, interactive educational games that require movement, such as augmented reality applications, can encourage children to explore their surroundings while learning. These tools can transform mundane learning tasks into exciting adventures, motivating children to move around, interact with peers, and immerse themselves in their environment. By selecting AI tools that incorporate physical movement, parents can ensure that their children remain active while still benefiting from technology.

Moreover, social interaction is a critical aspect of childhood development that can be fostered through intentional use of AI tools. Virtual platforms can facilitate connections among children who share similar interests, enabling them to collaborate on projects or engage in friendly competitions. Parents can encourage their children to use these platforms to form study groups or participate in online challenges that promote teamwork and social skills. By guiding children in using technology to build relationships, parents can help them develop vital interpersonal skills while also enhancing their learning experiences.

It is also essential for parents to set boundaries and create structured schedules that balance screen time with physical activity and social engagement. Designating specific times for using AI educational tools while ensuring ample time for outdoor activities, sports, or family games can help children develop a healthy lifestyle. Involving children in the planning process can empower them to take responsibility for their physical health and social interactions. By establishing these routines, parents can cultivate an environment where technology complements rather than replaces active play and social interaction.

Finally, leading by example is one of the most effective ways parents can encourage physical activity and social interaction. When children see their parents engaging in active pursuits, whether it be going for walks, playing sports, or participating in community events, they are more likely to emulate those behaviors. Parents can also organize family activities that involve both physical movement and social engagement, such as group outings to parks or sports events. By integrating these elements into everyday life, parents can create a positive atmosphere that values health, activity, and connection, ultimately enriching their children's learning experience in a holistic manner.

"Artificial intelligence is the future, and the future is here."
Fei-Fei Li

Chapter 8: The Future of AI in Education

Emerging Trends in AI Learning

The landscape of artificial intelligence in education is evolving rapidly, bringing forth innovative tools and methodologies that are reshaping how children learn. One of the most significant emerging trends is the integration of adaptive learning technologies. These systems leverage AI algorithms to assess a child's unique learning style and pace, tailoring educational content accordingly. This personalization not only enhances engagement but also fosters a deeper understanding of subjects, as the material is presented in a way that resonates with the individual learner. As parents, recognizing the benefits of adaptive learning can help you guide your child toward resources that cater to their specific needs.

Another noteworthy trend is the rise of gamification in educational platforms. By incorporating game-like elements, such as rewards, challenges, and interactive scenarios, these tools transform traditional learning into an engaging experience. This approach taps into children's natural inclination toward play, making complex concepts more accessible and enjoyable. As a parent, encouraging the use of gamified learning tools can motivate your child to embrace difficult subjects with enthusiasm, while also promoting critical thinking and critical thinking skills in a fun environment.

AI-driven analytics is also gaining traction in educational settings, providing valuable insights into a child's progress. These analytics can track performance metrics, identify areas of struggle, and suggest targeted interventions. For parents, this data offers a clearer picture of their child's learning journey and can inform discussions with teachers about personalized strategies for improvement. Understanding how to interpret these analytics can empower you to play an initiative-taking role in your child's education, ensuring they receive the support they need to succeed.

Collaboration tools powered by AI are another emerging trend that enhances learning experiences. These platforms facilitate communication between students, teachers, and parents, allowing for a more integrated approach to education. With features like real-time feedback and collaborative projects, children can develop essential social skills and teamwork abilities. By encouraging your child to participate in these collaborative learning environments, you can help them build a sense of community and connection, which is vital for their emotional and intellectual development.

Lastly, the use of virtual and augmented reality in education is on the rise, providing immersive experiences that can enrich learning. These technologies allow children to explore complex subjects in a firsthand manner, such as conducting virtual science experiments or exploring historical sites. As a parent, you can explore educational VR and AR tools that align with your child's interests, making learning an exciting adventure. Embracing these emerging trends in AI learning can equip your child with the skills and knowledge necessary for success in a rapidly changing world.

Preparing Children for an AI-Driven World

Preparing children for an AI-driven world involves equipping them with the skills and knowledge necessary to navigate and thrive in an increasingly technological landscape. Parents play a crucial role in this process, as they can guide their children in understanding the implications of artificial intelligence for their education and future careers. It is essential to foster a mindset that embraces technology while also encouraging critical thinking and creativity. This balanced approach will prepare children not only to use AI tools effectively but also to question and understand their impact.

One of the foundational aspects of preparing children for an AI-driven world is introducing them to the concept of AI itself. Parents can start by engaging in conversations that demystify artificial intelligence and its applications in everyday life. For instance, discussing how AI powers virtual assistants, recommendation systems, and even educational software can help children see the relevance of these technologies. By making these concepts accessible, parents can spark curiosity and encourage their children to explore how AI affects various fields, from healthcare to entertainment.

Incorporating AI-powered educational tools into daily learning routines can also significantly enhance a child's educational experience. Parents should evaluate different educational platforms that utilize AI to tailor learning experiences to individual needs. These tools often adapt to a child's learning pace and style, providing personalized feedback that can accelerate understanding. By actively participating in this learning process, parents can help their children develop adaptability and self-directed learning skills, which are vital in a world where AI is continually evolving.

Moreover, fostering a culture of inquiry and experimentation at home can prepare children for the complexities of an AI-driven environment. Encouraging them to ask questions, experiment with AI tools, and even participate in coding or robotics activities can nurture their problem-solving abilities. Parents can support this by providing resources such as books, online courses, or workshops that focus on technology and coding. This direct experience not only builds technical skills but also enhances creativity and resilience, preparing children to tackle challenges in innovative ways.

Lastly, it is crucial to emphasize the ethical considerations surrounding AI. As children become more adept at using AI tools, parents should engage them in discussions about privacy, bias, and the societal impacts of technology. Teaching children to think critically about these issues will not only prepare them to be responsible users of AI but also empower them to contribute to discussions on the future of technology. By instilling a sense of responsibility and ethical awareness, parents can help create a generation that is not only skilled in technology but also conscious of its implications.

Staying Informed and Involved as Parents

Staying informed and involved as parents in the context of AI-powered educational tools is crucial to fostering a supportive learning environment for children. The rapid evolution of technology presents both opportunities and challenges. Parents must educate themselves about the tools and resources available to their children, understanding how these technologies work and their implications for learning. By familiarizing themselves with AI-driven applications and platforms, parents can better guide their children in selecting appropriate tools that enhance their educational experiences.

Active participation in a child's learning journey is essential when utilizing AI tools. Parents should engage in conversations about what their children are learning and how AI technologies are being integrated into their education. This can involve asking questions about the specific applications being used, the content being explored, and the skills being developed. By showing interest and curiosity, parents not only reinforce the value of education but also encourage their children to articulate their learning experiences, fostering critical thinking and communication skills.

In addition to direct involvement, parents should also seek out resources and communities that focus on AI in education. Online forums, webinars, and local workshops can provide valuable insights into the latest developments in educational technology.

Networking with other parents and educators can create a support system where experiences and knowledge are shared. By connecting with a community dedicated to navigating the complexities of AI in education, parents can stay updated on best practices and emerging trends, ensuring they are well-equipped to support their children's learning.

Monitoring the effectiveness of AI educational tools is another vital aspect of parental involvement. Parents should regularly assess how these tools impact their children's learning outcomes, engagement levels, and overall academic progress. This may involve reviewing reports or feedback provided by the tools, as well as discussing performance with teachers. Being initiative-taking in evaluating the tools ensures that parents can make informed decisions about their continued use and can advocate for their children's needs if a particular technology is not serving them well.

Finally, fostering an open dialogue about technology use at home is essential. Parents should encourage their children to express their thoughts and feelings about the AI tools they engage in, promoting a critical understanding of technology's role in their lives. Discussing the balance between screen time and other activities, teaching children about digital citizenship and responsible use of technology, prepares them for the future. By staying informed and involved, parents can play a pivotal role in ensuring that AI-powered educational tools contribute positively to their child's learning experience, setting the stage for lifelong learning and adaptability in an increasingly digital world.

> *"The measure of intelligence is the ability to change."*
> **Albert Einstein**

The Author

Juan Ramon Rodulfo Moya, **Defined by Nature**: Inhabitant of Planet Earth, Human, Son of Eladio Rodulfo and Briceida Moya, Brother of Gabriela, Gustavo and Katiuska, Father of Gabriel and Sofia; **Defined by society**: Venezuelan Citizen (Limited Human Rights by default), Friend of many, enemy of few, Neighbor, Student/Teacher/Student, Worker/Supervisor/Manager/Leader/Worker, Husband of K/Ex-Husband of K/Husband of Y; **Defined by the U.S. Immigration Office**: Legal Alien; **Classroom studies**: Master's Degree in Human Resource Management, English, Mandarin Chinese; **Real-World Studies**: Human Behavior; **Home Studios**: SEO Webmaster, Graphic Design, Application and Website Development, Internet and Social Media Marketing, Video Production, YouTube Branding, Part 107 Commercial Drone Pilot, Import-Export, Affiliate Marketing, Cooking, Laundry, Home Cleaning; **Work experience**: Public-Private-Entrepreneurial Sectors; **Other definitions:** Bitcoin Evangelist, Human Rights, Peace and Love Advocate.

Publications:

Books:

- Why Maslow: How to use his theory to stay in Power Forever (EN/SP)
- Asylum Seekers (EN/SP)
- Manual for Gorillas: 9 Rules to be the "Fer-pect" Dictator (EN/SP)
- Why you must Play the Lottery (EN/SP); Para Español Oprima #2: Speaking Spanish in Times of Xenophobia (EN/SP)
- Cause of Death: IGNORANCE | Human Behavior in Times of PANIC (EN/SP)
- Politics explained for Millennials, GENs XYZ and future generations (EN/SP)
- Las cenizas del Ejército Libertador (EN/SP)
- Remain Silent: The only right we have. The legal Aliens (EN/SP)
- Fortune Cookie Coaching 88 Motivational Tips Made of Fortune Cookies, Vol I (EN)
- Vicky Erotic Tales, Vol I (EN)

Blogs:

Noticias de Nueva Esparta, Ubuntu Café, Coffee Secrets, Guaripete Pro, Rodulfox, Red

Wasp Drone, Barista Pro, Gorila Travel, Fortune Cookie Coach, All Books, Vicky Toys.

Audiovisual Productions:

Podcasts:

Ubuntu Cafe | Vicky Erotic Tales | Fortune Cookie Coach | All Books, available at: juanrodulfo.com/podcasts

Music:

Albums: Margarita | Race to Extinction | Relaxed Panda | Amazonia | Cassiopeia | Caracas | Arcoiris Musical | Close Your Eyes, available at: juanrodulfo.com/music

Photography & Video:

On sale at Adobe Stock, iStock, Shutterstock, and Veectezy, available at: juanrodulfo.com/gallery

Social Media Profiles:

Twitter / FB / Instagram / TikTok/ VK / LinkedIn / Sina Weibo: @rodulfox
Google Author: https://g.co/kgs/grjtN5
Google Artist: https://g.co/kgs/H7Fiqg

Twitter: https://twitter.com/rodulfox
Facebook: https://facebook.com/rodulfox
LinkedIn: https://www.linkedin.com/in/rodulfox
Instagram: https://www.instagram.com/rodulfox/
VK: https://vk.com/rodulfox
TikTok: https://www.tiktok.com/@rodulfox
Trading View: https://www.tradingview.com/u/rodulfox/

Table of Contents

Introduction 5
Chapter 1: Understanding AI in Education 9
How AI is Changing Learning 9
The Role of Parents in AI Education 12
Chapter 2: Choosing the Right AI Tools 15
Evaluating Educational Apps 15
Platforms for Personalized Learning 17
Safety and Privacy Considerations 20
Fun and Educational AI Tools for Kids to Use at Home 23
   1. AI-Powered Learning Assistants 23
   2. Creative AI Tools for Kids 24
   3. AI Coding & Robotics for Kids . 25
   4. AI Storytelling & Writing Helpers 26
Safety Tips for Parents Using AI with Kids: 27
Chapter 3: Integrating AI into Daily Learning 28
Setting Up a Learning Environment 28
Establishing a Routine with AI Tools 30
Encouraging Independent Learning 33

Chapter 4: Enhancing Learning with AI 36

Interactive Learning Experiences....36
Using AI for Homework Help....38
Gamification and Learning....41
Chapter 5: Supporting Diverse Learning Needs....44

AI for Different Learning Styles....44
Addressing Special Educational Needs....47
Language Learning with AI....49
Chapter 6: Monitoring Progress and Engagement....53

Tracking Learning Outcomes....53
Encouraging Feedback and Communication.55
Adjusting Tools Based on Performance....58
Chapter 7: Creating a Balanced Approach 61

Limiting Screen Time....61
Combining Traditional Learning with AI....64
How to Combine Traditional Learning with AI Tools for Kids at Home....67
  1. Reinforce Reading & Writing with AI Assistance....67
  2. Enhance Math Skills with AI & Hands-On Practice....68
  3. Blend Science Experiments with AI Exploration....69
  4. Combine Art & Creativity with AI Inspiration....70

5. Develop Critical Thinking with AI & Real-World Discussions 70

6. Balance Screen Time with Offline Learning 71

Encouraging Physical Activity and Social Interaction 72

Chapter 8: The Future of AI in Education 76

Emerging Trends in AI Learning 76
Preparing Children for an AI-Driven World .. 78
Staying Informed and Involved as Parents 81
The Author 87

Publications: 88
    Books: 88
    Blogs: 88

Audiovisual Productions: 89
    Podcasts: 89

    Music: 89

    Photography & Video: 89

Social Media Profiles: 89